Bringing Solvency To Social Security

Bringing Solvency To Social Security

A Solution For Future Generations
The Series SS Bond

Charles Gordon

iUniverse, Inc.
New York Lincoln Shanghai

Bringing Solvency To Social Security
A Solution For Future Generations
The Series SS Bond

iUniverse books may be ordered through booksellers or by contacting:

iUniverse
2021 Pine Lake Road, Suite 100
Lincoln, NE 68512
www.iuniverse.com
1-800-Authors (1-800-288-4677)

ISBN-13: 978-0-595-35674-4 (pbk)
ISBN-13: 978-0-595-80151-0 (ebk)
ISBN-10: 0-595-35674-5 (pbk)
ISBN-10: 0-595-80151-X (ebk)

Printed in the United States of America

Contents

Isn't Anyone The Least Bit Curious?

It was never my intention to have to write a book, to get out to the public, my plan to bring solvency to Social Security. I am not a book writer. Realistically, I do not expect this writing *exercise* to get to fifty pages. Maybe it won't even be classified as a book. Will I be able to find a publisher to send it to print? Quite possibly, I could be the *only* person who will be impressed with, and see value in, this writing endeavor. I am hoping though, that I am not the only person who appreciates writing that is "concise," "to the point," "short and sweet," and "not wasteful of paper."

The real reason for proceeding on this path, of writing a book, is that I have not been very successful in getting anyone to listen to my proposal. Back in December of 2004, I sent a brief letter to Howard Dean. I wrote to tell him that I had a solution for making Social Security solvent. As someone who was fighting for the chairmanship of the Democratic Party, I thought that he might find it *useful* to have this kind of information. I received a response from Governor Dean within a couple of weeks. It was a very nice form letter, which started out, "Thank you for your support." There was *no* mention of any *interest* in my Plan. I figured that all of Governor Dean's efforts, at the time, were being channeled into trying to win the DNC chairmanship, and not with addressing national issues. I concluded that it was bad timing on my part.

Next, I wrote and faxed a letter to Senator Clinton. Again, I wrote that I had a Plan to bring solvency to Social Security.

This time, there was no response at all. I reasoned that her office might receive 200 or more communications every day of the year. Would this letter be viewed as one that was worthy of a response? I can only suppose that my letter might have been considered a foolish prank. I still expect to receive a letter from the Senator's office some day stating, "Thank you for your support."

My third and final letter went out to the American Association of Retired Persons. Social Security is a front-page issue for the AARP. Because of their stance on Social Security, the AARP has been under attack by various political action groups. I made a phone call to the AARP offices and got their fax number. I drafted a new letter for the Executive Director of the AARP. I sent a message similar to the others, explaining that I had a Plan to bring solvency to Social Security. It has now been quite a few weeks since I sent the fax and there has been no response. Having received no inquiries from any of the letters I had sent, I was left with a feeling of *quiet* aggravation.

Many of you who are reading this, have already concluded, that I have been trying to contact the wrong people. You are thinking that my efforts have been met with inaction because I did not contact any of the real people in political power...the Republicans.

Well, let me tell you about my perceived risk in contacting the Republicans. Some of you may not agree, but this is how I see it. This is *my* reality. None of the Republicans in Congress are going to react favorably toward a plan that opposes the White House. And we all know that the White House is calling for privatization, or "private accounts," when it comes to dealing with Social Security. I personally, oppose taking money out of the Social Security Trust Fund and putting it into private accounts. This opposition stems from the fact that money placed in private accounts would be controlled by, and would primarily benefit, the financial services industry. Here is what I could foresee happening to my plan, if given to the Republicans. I envision that they would take the idea, and then *bury* it in a legislative landfill. Some of you will say that this is paranoid thinking, and others will say that it really *could* happen. Therefore, I thought that it would be too *risky* to attempt to gain support from Republicans. It was *my* choice and *my* decision. I therefore decided, that I was going to write directly to the American people. I believe they will understand that my plan will lead to what most people think is the best "solution" to the problem facing Social Security. The *best* solution, of course, lies in the issue of *solvency*. My plan deals exclusively with solvency, which means that the American people will ultimately benefit, and not the aforementioned financial services industry. I am proposing "supplemental" funding of the

Social Security Trust Fund with a new type of bond. The following section deals with specific details of my Plan. I hope that you will find my Bond Plan to be a viable alternative to the White House plan for private accounts.

Plan Features Of The Series SS Bond

I. The Series SS Bond is a low yield bond similar to the Series EE Bond.

II. The Series SS Bond is purchased at full face value, in denominations of $25, $50, $100, $500, $1000, $5000, and $10000.

III. The Series SS Bond is deductible from your federal income taxes at 100% of face value. It is not deductible from city and state income taxes.

IV. The purchaser may buy for him/herself up to $10000 per year in Series SS Bonds.

V.   The purchaser may buy up to $10000 in Series SS Bonds for any other American citizen, for each and every calendar year. There is no limit on the number of persons these bonds can be purchased for. For example, a grandparent can purchase up to $10000 per year in Series SS Bonds for every grandchild they have.

VI.   Private corporations can purchase Series SS Bonds for employees and receive the federal tax deduction.

VII.   All money from purchases of Series SS Bonds will go into a separate Social Security Trust Fund account that cannot be used for any purpose other than payment of Social Security benefits.

VIII. Series SS Bonds can be purchased from commercial banks, just as Series EE Bonds. Order forms will be in quadruplicate, with one form to accompany the money to the U.S. Treasury or other government agency; one form to stay with the bank; and two forms will be given to the purchaser. The purchaser will send one validated form with his/her income tax return, and the fourth form will be retained in their personal files.

IX.   Series SS Bonds will not be redeemable for six years.

X.   Series SS Bonds redeemed before age 62 will require a 25% early redemption penalty payment.

XI.   Series SS Bonds can be redeemed at commercial banks just as Series EE Bonds. The 25% early redemption penalty fee will be deducted at the time of redemption.

XII.   The early redemption penalty fee will be retained in the Social Security Trust Fund.

XIII. Redeemed Series SS Bonds will be taxed as regular income on the federal income tax return.

XIV. Redeemed Series SS Bonds will not be subject to State and City income taxes.

XV. The purchaser of Series SS Bonds will use Line 27 of "Schedule A-Itemized Deductions" to report Series SS Bond purchases and will attach a validated copy of the Series SS Bond Order Form to the Schedule A.

XVI. Private corporations will report Series SS Bond purchases in a similar manner and submit validated Series SS Bond Order Forms with their federal income tax returns.

XVII. The Series SS Bond is transferable to a designated beneficiary upon the death of the bond's owner.

A Discussion of Solvency

The Series SS Bond addresses two primary solvency issues. The first is that money from the purchase of Series SS Bonds is extra money (in excess of payroll taxes) being paid directly into the Social Security Trust Fund.

Let's do some simple arithmetic. If 10 million people purchase just one $10000 Series SS Bond, the Social Security Trust Fund gains $100 Billion. Add 10 million people purchasing one $1000 Series SS Bond and the SS Trust Fund gains another $10 Billion. Now add 10 million people purchasing one $500 Series SS Bond and you gain $5 Billion. Add 10 million people purchasing one $100 Series SS Bond and you gain $1 Billion. Add 10 million people purchasing one $50 Series SS Bond and you gain $500 Million. And now add 10 million people purchasing one $25 Series SS Bond and you gain another $250 Million. When you add all of these purchases, for ONE year, you have added an extra $116.75 Billion to the Social Security Trust Fund. After the first six years of Series SS Bond purchases, when no bonds are redeemable, the SS Trust Fund will have accumulated an extra $700.5 Billion.

With some advertising, and a push by the media, these projections could be set significantly higher. My example does not even include any contributions from private corporations. If you have not come to a definitive conclusion yet, your interest and excitement for this plan should at least be slightly elevated!

The second solvency issue involves individuals. The Series SS Bond owner, actually has in their possession, extra money that will be used by him or her during their retirement. The Bonds will be income for them, in addition to a monthly Social Security check.

Under the present system, Social Security is funded through payroll taxes. Obviously, if you are not working you are not contributing to the Social Security Trust Fund. With the Series SS Bond plan, the dynamics for making payments into the SS Trust Fund will be drastically changed and dramatically increased.

My plan will draw countless millions of extra contributors to the Social Security Trust Fund. A 10 year-old child could save and use his allowance or birthday money to purchase a Series SS Bond. A retired grandparent, who is not working, who understands the need for retirement income, can purchase the Series SS Bond for their grandchildren. A wife or husband could purchase a Series SS Bond for each other. A father or mother can purchase the Series SS Bond for their own child, or a child can purchase the Series SS Bond for their father or mother.

Then, there are the possible contributions from private corporations. The Series SS Bond plan could be used as all, or part of a corporation's employee retirement benefit. Pension plans could be made obsolete.

Also, I believe employees would enjoy knowing that their retirement plan has been prepaid and pre-delivered. Many people are concerned that Social Security benefits will not be available for them when they retire. Well, just think for a moment of the thousands of Americans who have had their pensions squandered, and lost by the corporations that they have worked for. With the Series SS Bond plan, an employee will have immediate possession of their future retirement money.

How great do you think this sounds to millions of employees who have ended up with nothing after countless years of faithful service to a company? And just think of how little paperwork would be involved with the Series SS Bond plan.

Series SS Bonds can be purchased for as little as $25, thus making them affordable to almost all Americans. They will be the poor man's IRA. There are no custodial fees and no transaction fees.

The Series SS Bond is safe, simple, and secure. If your family budget is stretched to the max, and you do not have extra money for the purchase of Series SS Bonds, you do not have to worry. Social Security will still be there for you. And wealthier Americans will be there to pick up the slack with the purchase of Series SS Bonds. Their purchases, and in fact, all purchases of the Series SS Bonds will strengthen the *entire* Social Security System. The Series SS Bond plan allows those with extra money to save more for their future, but in doing so, the Social Security System as a whole will be strengthened. And this will benefit both the poor, and the not so poor.

The Politics of Social Security

Now, let's talk politics. All Americans should be alerted to the fact that the Bush plan for privatization, creating individual private accounts, actually reduces payments into the Social Security Trust Fund. This will ultimately, and quite possibly almost immediately, weaken the Social Security System and threaten the ability of the System to pay recipient benefits. We are not just talking about retirement benefits. We are also talking about putting in jeopardy the payment to millions of Americans who now rely on disability checks from Social Security.

It is not inconceivable, to conclude that the entire Social Security system could collapse in just a few short years if the Bush plan is implemented. So, why is Bush proposing such a plan? Why would he imply that his plan for creating private accounts would strengthen Social Security, when in fact it would do just the opposite?

Let's look at the politics of the issue, with a specific emphasis of following the "money trail." Bush was speaking to an organization of African-Americans a couple of months ago, and he said that with his plan for private accounts, "you could not play the lottery and you could not play dice games with the money". It was interesting to me, to hear Bush explain that you could not *gamble* away your private account money on the lottery or dice games. I think we can all assume though, that it is "perfectly acceptable" for all of us to *gamble* away our private account money on the stock market.

We all know how hard Bush is pushing private accounts, but just where does the money go when you establish a private account with your Social Security money? The truth is, that you must put the money into an account managed by a private company in the financial services industry. You should understand that you are not going to physically get your hands on this money. There is a "middle man." And most of us know about the middle man. He is going to want his *share*. And the financial services industry, which is the middle man in this scheme, is going to get *more* than his fair share. Merrill Lynch, JP Morgan Chase, Bank of America, Citigroup, and many other companies are all going to have their hands in the cookie jar. Obviously, the cookie jar will *not* be filled with cookies. It will be filled with billions of dollars of hard-earned social security money….*your* hard-earned money.

Bush has repeatedly stated that the American people should be able to invest their social security money in the stock market. We have all seen and heard the messages in the media from the financial services industry. One message that I have seen, involves an example of how much money you can earn over a 25 or 30-year period if you invest in the stock market and earn "8 percent" a year. It is a lot of money. You never hear anyone ask however, if that 8 percent is "guaranteed." If it is "guaranteed," then I'll sign up, right now! But guess what, it is just an *enticing* example. This "8 percent" return on investment is not guaranteed. Actually, because of ethics' issues, a stock broker *cannot* make claims of a "guarantee" on returns from stock purchases.

Now, to be somewhat fair on this issue, there are people who *have* made 8 percent returns on their stock market investments. Some have made even higher returns. The fact remains however, that investments in the stock market are a gamble. How many people are willing to, or can afford to, gamble away their retirement income?

Rich people can probably afford to take the risk. Then, there are the "risk takers." We have all met the risk takers. They are a rare breed. Some have had great success, and I can honestly say that I envy some of them. But let's face up to reality, there are many risk takers who fail. What are these people going to do when they wake up one day and realize that their social security money has been lost?

If Bush rams through this plan for private accounts, it guarantees that the Social Security Trust Fund will go bust much sooner than if we stay the course with the present system. That means that we will all be forced to take the gamble, and start a private account, because we will need to supplement a *failed* Social Security System.

Here is what is going to happen to thousands of these new American "investors," who will sign up for the "private account plan." First, there may be a fee just to "open" the account. Then, you will learn that there are maintenance or custodial fees. These are generally paid on a yearly basis. The "custodian" will probably have the right to *automatically* deduct the fee from your account. Next, there will be transaction fees. If you buy a stock, there will be a fee. If you sell a stock, there will be a fee. And guess what, it doesn't matter if you have made a profit on the stock or lost money, the transaction fee still must be paid.

Losing money from stock and mutual funds is always a difficult matter to deal with. There is however, a worse demise and a greater horror that awaits you in this gambling casino, called the stock market. What, you are wondering, could be worse than losing money? Well, it's this; having to *interact* with your stock broker, who is sometimes referred to as an investment *advisor*. Here is one scenario that many previous investors will be able to confirm. You will first set up your account and make your first purchase of Stock XYZ. Then, a few months later, you will get a call from your investment advisor. He/she has a "hot tip," "a once in a lifetime opportunity," "a chance to get in on a ground-floor opportunity," or "a chance to make some big, easy money." You explain that you do not have any more money, in this case "private account" money, available this year to purchase Stock ABC. Your investment advisor suggests selling Stock XYZ, and then buying Stock ABC. The salesmanship of the investment advisor is *overwhelming* and you give in, and agree to follow their advice. It is possible that you have put yourself in a better investment position. We can't really be certain at this point in time.

What we can be certain of though, is that your investment advisor has *improved* his/her position. He/she has made a commission on the original purchase of Stock XYZ, a commission on the sale of Stock XYZ, and then completes the trifecta with the commission on the purchase of Stock ABC.

If there are any readers out there who have invested, and can honestly say that this has never happened to them, you are one of the lucky ones. I would guess that for every person who has not had this type of experience, there are at least one hundred who would say that it *has* happened to them. It has happened to me. The ultimate, nightmare scenario is of course, when the investment advisor "churns" an account and the investor actually ends up owing more money to the investment company than they originally invested. Advice comes in two forms....good and bad. Unfortunately, when dealing with money, bad advice can be quite painful, both financially and emotionally.

I would hope that everyone now has a better sense of what is driving Bush to push for private accounts. Shortly after the 2004 elections, Bush said that he had "earned political capital," and he was going to *spend* it. I found this statement to be quite disingenuous. To me, this man had won the election by a rather narrow margin.

Now, he was up on his pulpit and crowing about a supposed mandate, and a reform program that will *probably* destroy Social Security. In my way of thinking, when a politician gets elected to office, it is time for him to "pay back" all of the people and organizations who paid money into his campaign, and who actively went out on the campaign trail and helped get him elected. In the case of Bush, the financial services industry contributed millions of dollars to his election campaign. Having been elected, it is now time for Bush to acknowledge this help, and *pay back* the financial services industry. Bush could do this by bringing forth a plan to *supposedly reform* Social Security by establishing private accounts. The financial services industry is standing first in line to benefit from this proposal by being the caretakers and custodians of these accounts. Just follow the money trail. What goes around, will come around. The financial services industry invested heavily in the Bush election campaign, and now it is time for Bush to *deliver* a big return on investment, to this industry.

Bush is admitting, along with many experts, that his plan does not address the impending insolvency issue facing Social Security. He also must admit that his plan takes money *out* of the Social Security System. So, why would Americans be better off with *his* plan? Why should hard-working Americans, who opt for private accounts, knowing that they will receive greatly reduced payments from Social Security, be pushed into thinking that they will automatically be better off financially when they retire? Remember, there are no guarantees from returns on stock market investments.

Listen to me, my fellow Americans, the Bush plan is a "sell-out" to the financial services industry. Once again, Bush is betraying the trust of many Americans. We expect our President to look out for, and do what is right for, all of the "little people" in this great country. We expect our President to make decisions that will benefit a majority of Americans, especially the little people. But this President is turning his back on the little people and selling us out to Big Business. There is no mistake about it, Bush is selling out to the financial services industry and his plan for private accounts is going to leave us little people, in a *worse* financial situation. He is going to *gut* the Social Security System that so many Americans rely on, especially the little people, and it is going to bring poverty to the doorstep of millions.

We have all heard it said about Bush that, "he says what he means, and he means what he says." I don't want to hear this anymore, from anyone. What we are now finding out about this man is that he says what his advisors are telling him to say. His thoughts are not his own. After all, he is a politician. And what he "means" is just a contrived bunch of ideas concocted by his advisors. And what he means, we are finding out, is that his "reform" of Social Security does not mean helping a majority of Americans.

In fact, his private accounts plan for allegedly reforming Social Security is a betrayal of the trust of a majority of Americans. His plan benefits large corporations and hurts the little people of this country. The little people of this country need to be helped and protected in retirement, and the Bush plan will drive many people to starvation and poverty.

The Bush legacy is now being written, and we have heard what he has said, and we now know what he means. Bush is again using "scare tactics," this time to change the Social Security System. And we all know what these changes will mean. The money from the private account plan will be given to, and controlled by Bush's rich friends, who are executives in the finance and investment industry. By keeping this money from being deposited in the Social Security Trust Fund, the Social Security System will surely collapse.

So there, the Bush legacy has been written. Bush will have betrayed a vast majority of Americans, but he will have *helped* his friends in the finance and investment industry. Bush will be proud though, of this legacy, because he will be told that he *should* be proud. He will have been told this, by that small group of advisors that keep him isolated from outside opinion.

This man is actually starring in a modern day version of "The Emperor's New Clothes." In the original story, the Emperor is lead to believe that he is wearing beautiful new clothes, but in reality he is only in his underwear. This is the way it is with Bush. He is a man, I have heard, who does not watch television and does not read newspapers. He knows therefore, only what his advisors tell him. I believe, this is probably the reason why millions of people in this country and the world, see this man in a state of nakedness. Decisions have been made that seem to be devoid of practical and ethical considerations. It has been difficult at times, to believe that an *American* President is making some of the decisions that have been made.

Furthermore, when Bush leaves the White House and talks to groups of people, as he is now with Social Security, who is actually sitting in the audience? It is an audience that has been screened by Bush advisors. If you are a Bush supporter, one who is in total agreement with him, you are let into the event to be a part of the audience.

Then, when the question and answer phase of the event begins, all questions have been screened and pre-selected, and Bush is tutored on how to respond. How disingenuous of Bush. After the 2004 election, Karl Rove, the "architect" of the Bush fabrication, said in an interview that Bush was "intellectually gifted." I am sure Mr. Rove that your Emperor was listening. Bush says that he wants to engage the American public in a dialogue about Social Security, but what do we get? We get *only* the Bush viewpoint.

Again, the Bush legacy is being written. And again, it is a legacy of deceit and dishonesty. The American people will have to put up with Bush for over three more years. But in 2006, I would hope that the American people will have come to their senses and vote out of office the Bush supporters in Congress. I am not saying vote *out* all Republicans and vote *in* all Democrats. There are some Republicans who realize that the Bush plan for private accounts is wrong. It is crucial, to do your homework and make an informed decision.

Final Thoughts

Having rambled on about the politics of the Social Security issue, it is now time to refocus. I have always said that I believe I live in the "real" world. The reality of the matter is; there can be no reform of Social Security without going through the political process.

Here is where we stand, America. A majority of people believe that the Social Security System *needs help*. A majority of people believe that the Bush plan is *wrong*. A majority of Republicans in the Congress seem to be willing to follow the President. But, will they follow, if it means political suicide?

I have proposed the establishment of a "supplemental" payment system that will lead to solvency in the Social Security System. Everything else will stay in place. Payroll taxes will stay in place. The $90,000 cap will stay in place. And most importantly, recipient benefits will stay in place. Most of the experts speaking on the issue, including many of the talking heads on television, say that the Bush plan does not address solvency. The establishment of the Series SS Bond plan directly addresses this issue. It is in fact, the *heart and soul* of the plan.

Next, there is the issue that Bush seems to want to embrace, and that is, private ownership of wealth. No one is *against* accumulating wealth. However, when you are talking about reducing payments into the Social Security Trust Fund, this would be Wrong. Bush will never be able to understand why this is Wrong, because he is rich and will never have to rely on Social Security for retirement income. There are certain aspects of the system that may not seem equitable, but these are the things that make the system work.

Some people work and pay into the SS system for 40 years, retire, and then receive Social Security checks for another 30 years. They will receive more than they pay in. There is also the worker who works for 40 years and dies within the first year of retiring. This person doesn't get much in return, personally, but a surviving spouse may get a benefit check.

Life can be cruel, but the Social Security System has been in place for many decades because all people do not work for 40 years and then collect Social Security checks for another 30 years. The system would have been broke a long time ago if this were the case. My plan, the Series SS Bond Plan, allows for some *extra* personal savings incentives for all workers, be they rich, or poor. For as little as $25 you can buy a little extra future retirement income, and you will actually hold this asset in your possession. It will also be an asset that will be transferable, upon your death, to a designated beneficiary.

Ultimately, I believe Americans will give tremendous support to the Series SS Bond Plan. It will help keep alive a great American institution, The Social Security System. I believe the purchase of these bonds will be viewed as being very PATRI-OTIC. Purchasing Series SS Bonds will become a very AMERICAN thing to do. Americans will purchase Series SS Bonds to strengthen Social Security just as Americans bought War Bonds to support our country during World War II.

Now, let's get back to politics. There is the optimistic part of me that is thinking "game, set, and match. The Social Security crisis is over. Let's move on to the next problem facing America." But then, I feel the negative, pessimistic part of me taking an overwhelming grip around my neck and I know that there is genuine cause for concern.

Will the politicians choke the lifeblood out of this idea and kill it? If I were to use George Tenet's magic phrase "it's a slam dunk" to describe my plan, do you think Bush would suddenly end support for his private accounts plan and support the Series SS Bond Plan? Let's face it, Bush and his Republican backers are not going to suddenly abandon the private accounts plan and go away quietly. We have all seen how their pompous, arrogant, self-righteous attitudes have lead this country down the *wrong* path on other issues.

As for the Democrats, they believe the Republicans are making themselves vulnerable on the private accounts issue, and they sense this could give Democratic candidates a political advantage in the 2006 elections. So, why should the Democrats endorse my Series SS Bond plan when it will completely *diffuse* the Social Security issue, thus closing the door on their grand scheme to pick up seats in Congress, in 2006? No, I'm not feeling too good about getting my Plan implemented. After all, it only helps the little people of America. Politicians say that, "they are always looking out for the little guy." Well, I have just one thing say to those politicians... PROVE IT!

Bush says he wants to take the debate to the American people. That sounds just fine to me, let's debate my Plan. There is however, one thing that I would have to agree with Democrats. Private accounts have to come *off* the table, first and foremost! I still have serious reservations about whether Republicans and Democrats will work harmoniously together in solving the problems with Social Security. The essence of the body politic is antagonistic and adversarial. So, let's sweeten the pot. I know that many will instantly conclude that what I am about to say is an extremely outrageous assumption, but I have nothing to lose, except maybe a *little* credibility. At least, I can honestly say that I am trying to help the American people, and I fervently believe that my Series SS Bond Plan will do just that.

I believe the Series SS Bond Plan will make Social Security solvent, in perpetuity. I also believe that it is possible that there could be sufficient money left over to help with the impending funding crisis in Medicare and Medicaid. Of primary importance to me, is to first implement my Series SS Bond Plan to help fund Social Security. However, if there should be enough money to also provide supplemental funding to Medicare and Medicaid, then I would also support that *usage* of the money.

I also think that it would be in everyone's best interest to watch upcoming "Series SS Bond" legislation, very closely. I suppose that I should interject, at this point in time, that I am "hopeful" that my Bond Plan will be legislated. The Republicans though, may *seize* the opportunity and the money from the Bond Plan to use it for other purposes. They might use it to buy down the HUGE budget deficit that they have brought to this country.

Though it may be a bit condescending, I would have to say to the Republicans, who control the Congress, that this would be a "No, No." The Republicans have spent a lot of money, and created huge debt for this country, in the past few years. They have been acting like irresponsible teenagers who have been given a credit card, with no limit, and then let free to go on a shopping spree at the mall. Maybe the Republicans still do have something to *worry* about in 2006.

Problems and Solutions

A few short pages of this writing endeavor are devoted to identifying a problem, and then offering a solution to that problem. All of the rest of the pages seem to be filled with a rather cynical and pessimistic view of how things are going in this country. That is especially noted, when it comes to *who* is in charge, and the decisions that are being made. My plan, the Series SS Bond Plan, is a very serious attempt to address the solvency issue for Social Security. I believe it is a credible Plan. It is a very simple solution to a very complex and monumentally important problem that is facing our great nation.

I am proud that I am attempting to do something that will help so many people. I believe that Social Security is a great American institution and every effort should be made to keep it strong, and keep it going. It is a safety net for millions of Americans. It is important that it be kept going, forever and ever. I cannot know at this time if my plan will be legislated, but I know that it is a viable, alternative to the President's plan for "private accounts."

I am just one of those little people that I have already talked about. I can only imagine that there are a lot of other little people, who may also have an idea that will solve a problem facing our country. If you run into difficulty in getting anyone to listen, be patient, and be persistent.

In closing, I would like to leave you with a personal sentiment, a wish for everyone in this great country. May you all have a *long* journey to a *prosperous* retirement!

978-0-595-35674-4
0-595-35674-5